THIS COLORING BOOK BELONGS TO:

█ █ █ █ █ █ █ █ █ █ █ █ █ █ █ █ █ █ █ █

I0491983

If lost, please return to:

Full name: ----------------------------------

Adress: ----------------------------------

Email: ----------------------------------

This children's coloring book is full of beautiful Cute Robots, funny illustrations; over 26 Designs to Color

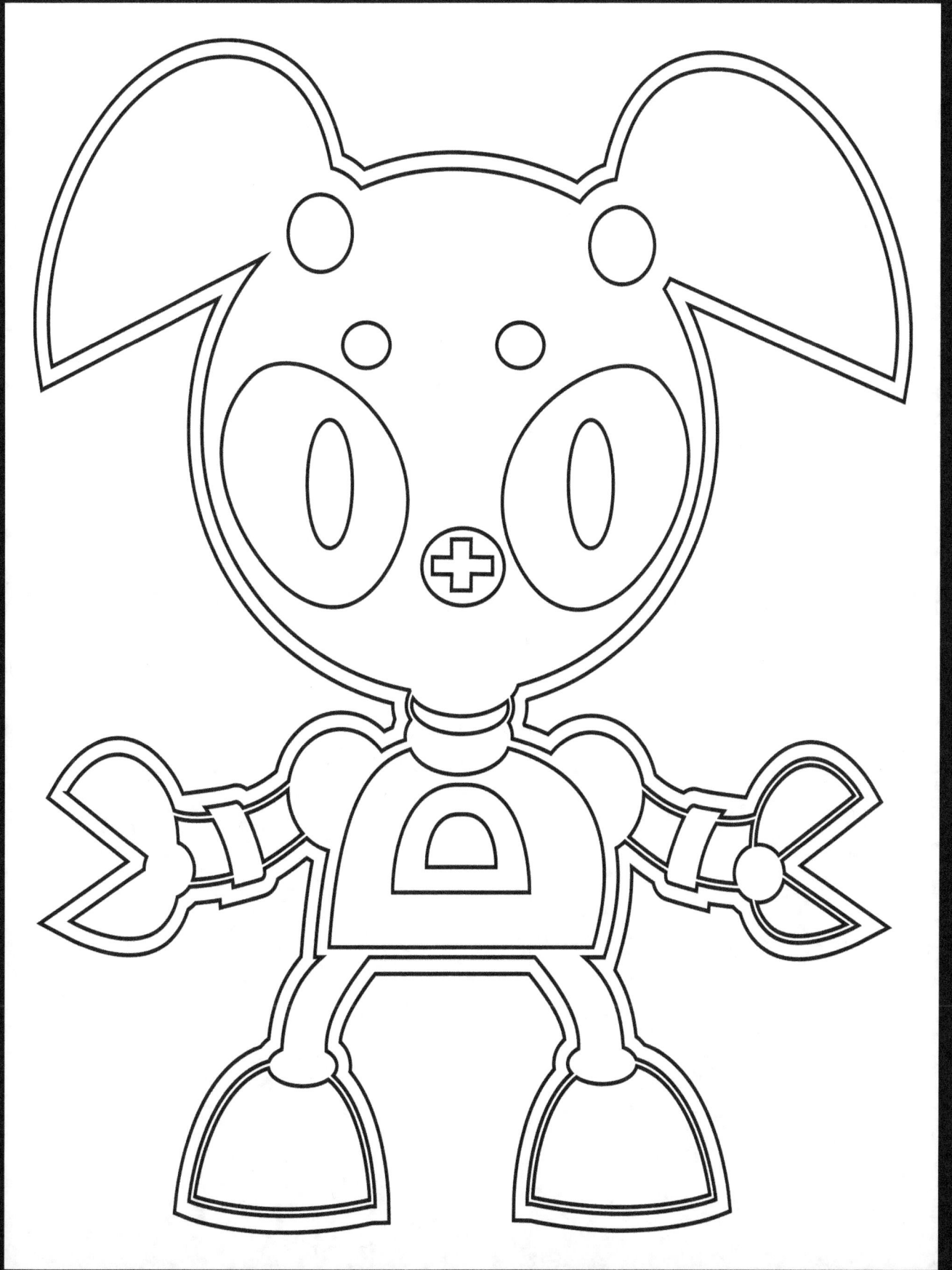

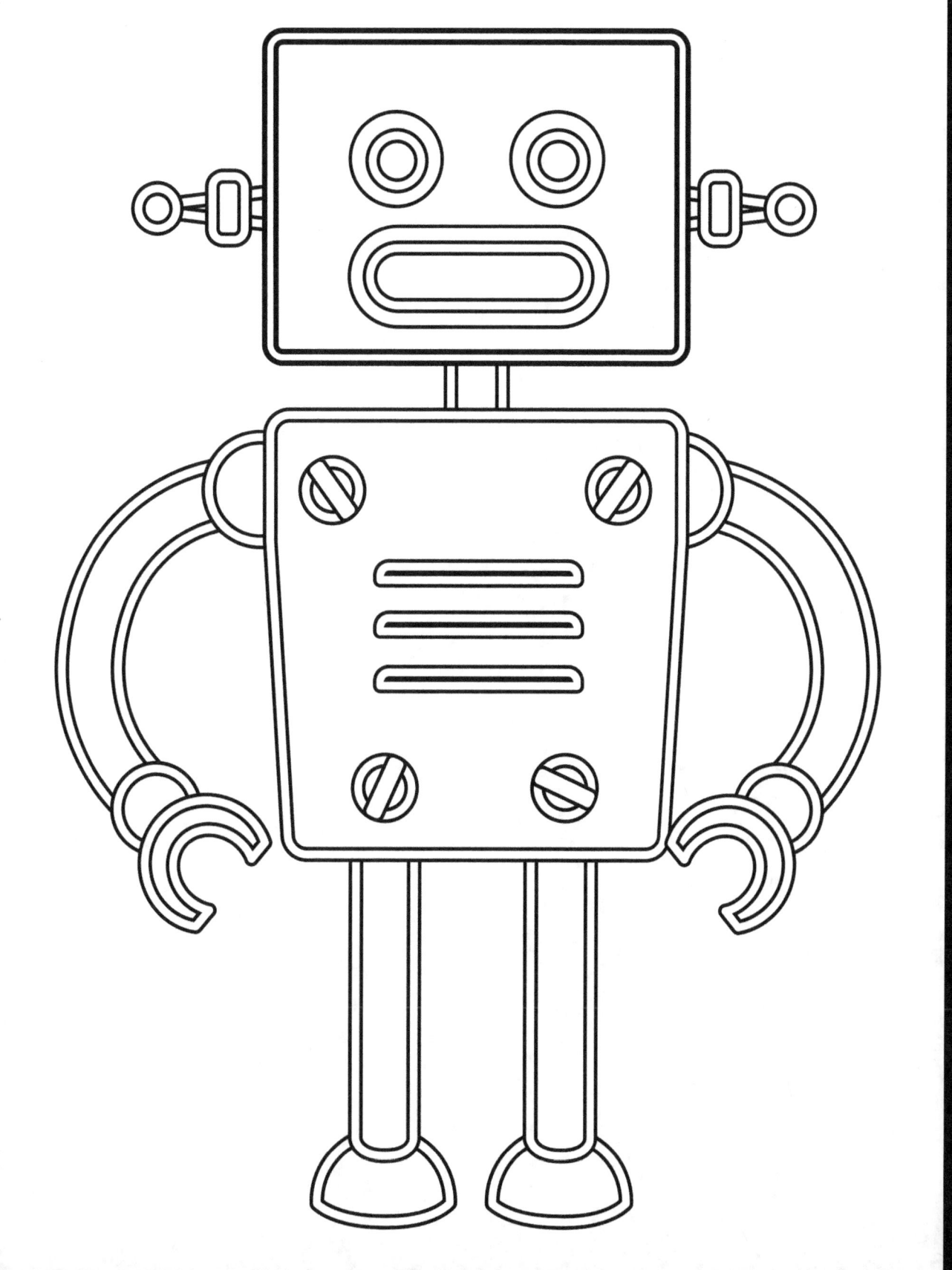

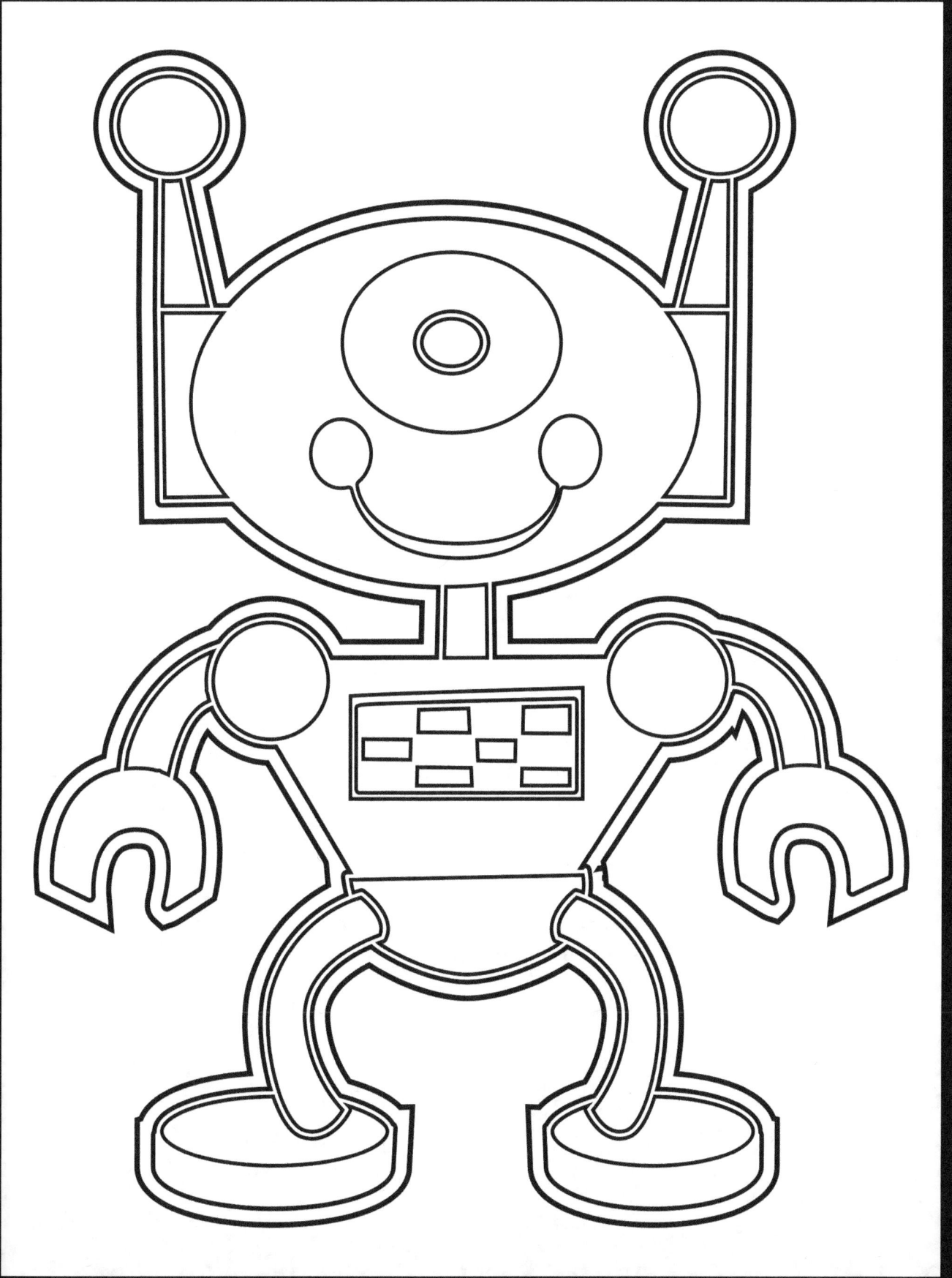

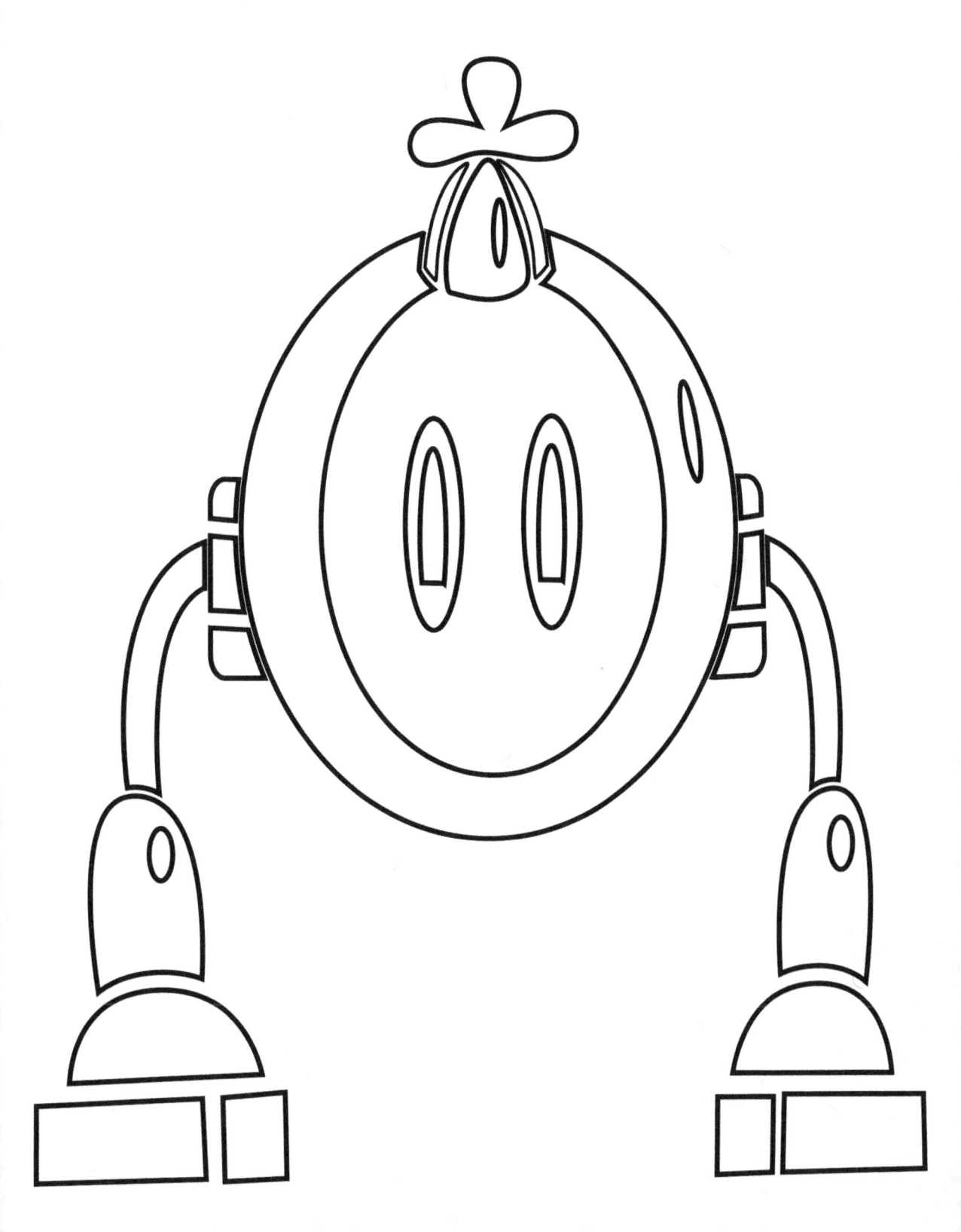

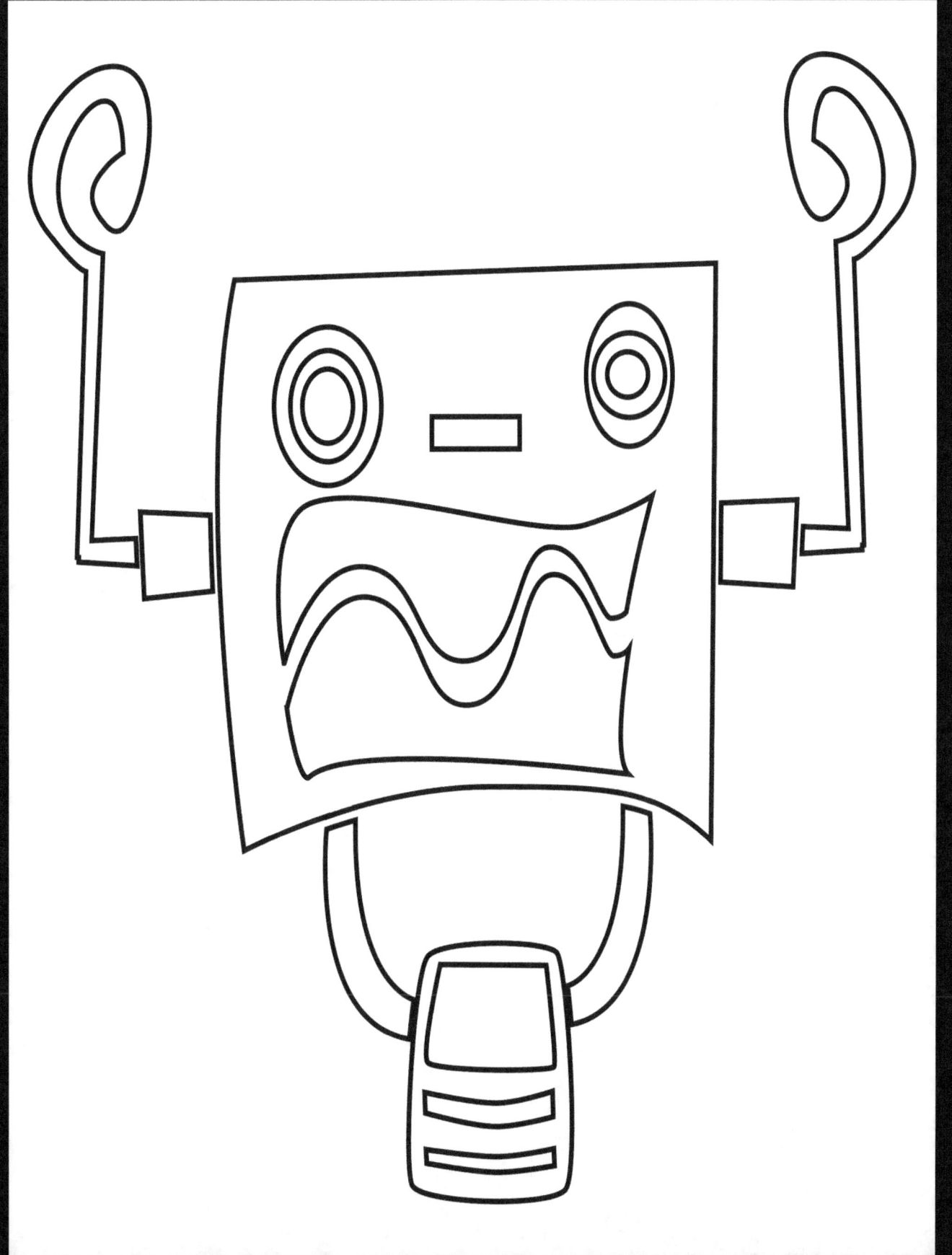

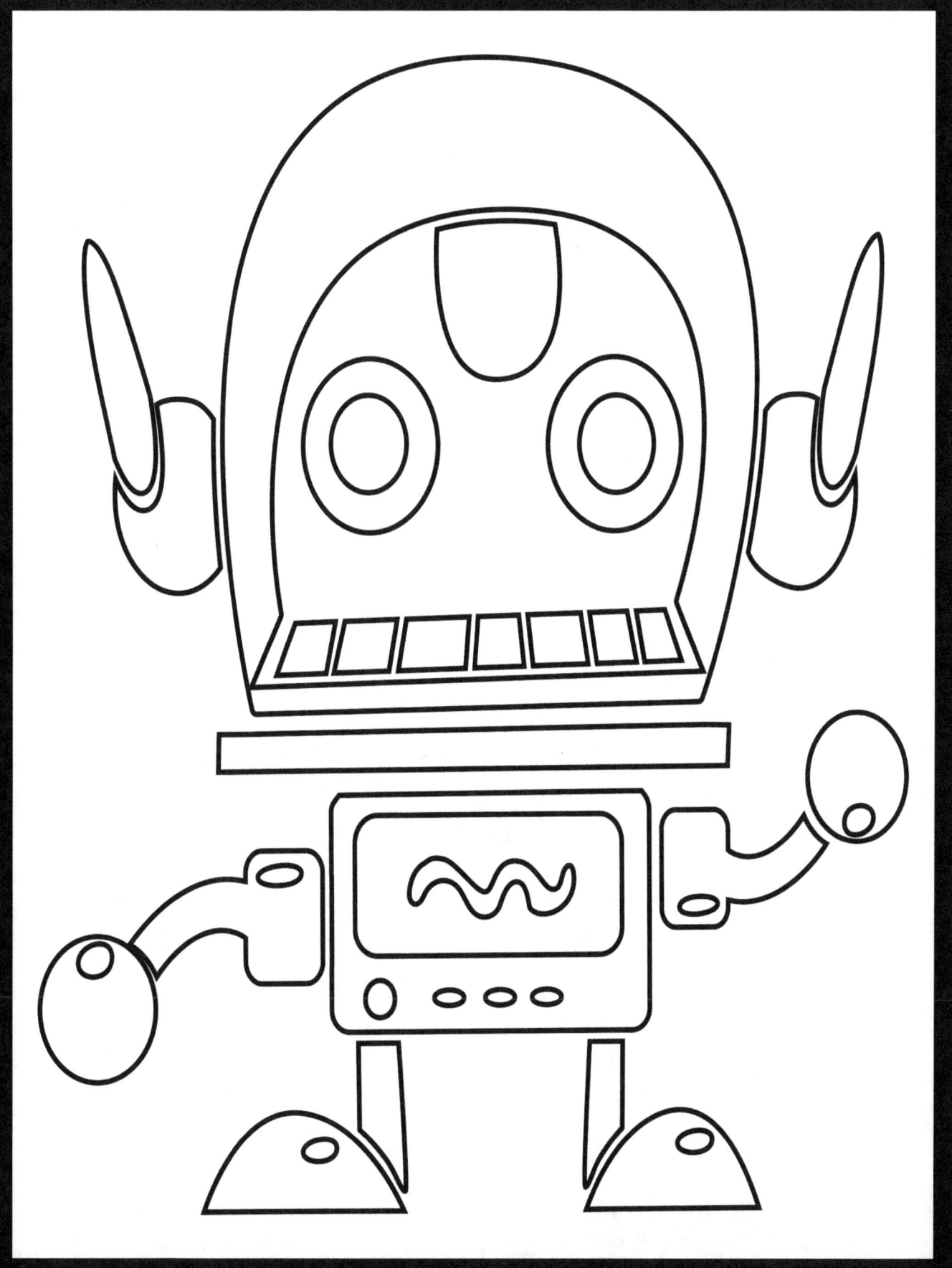

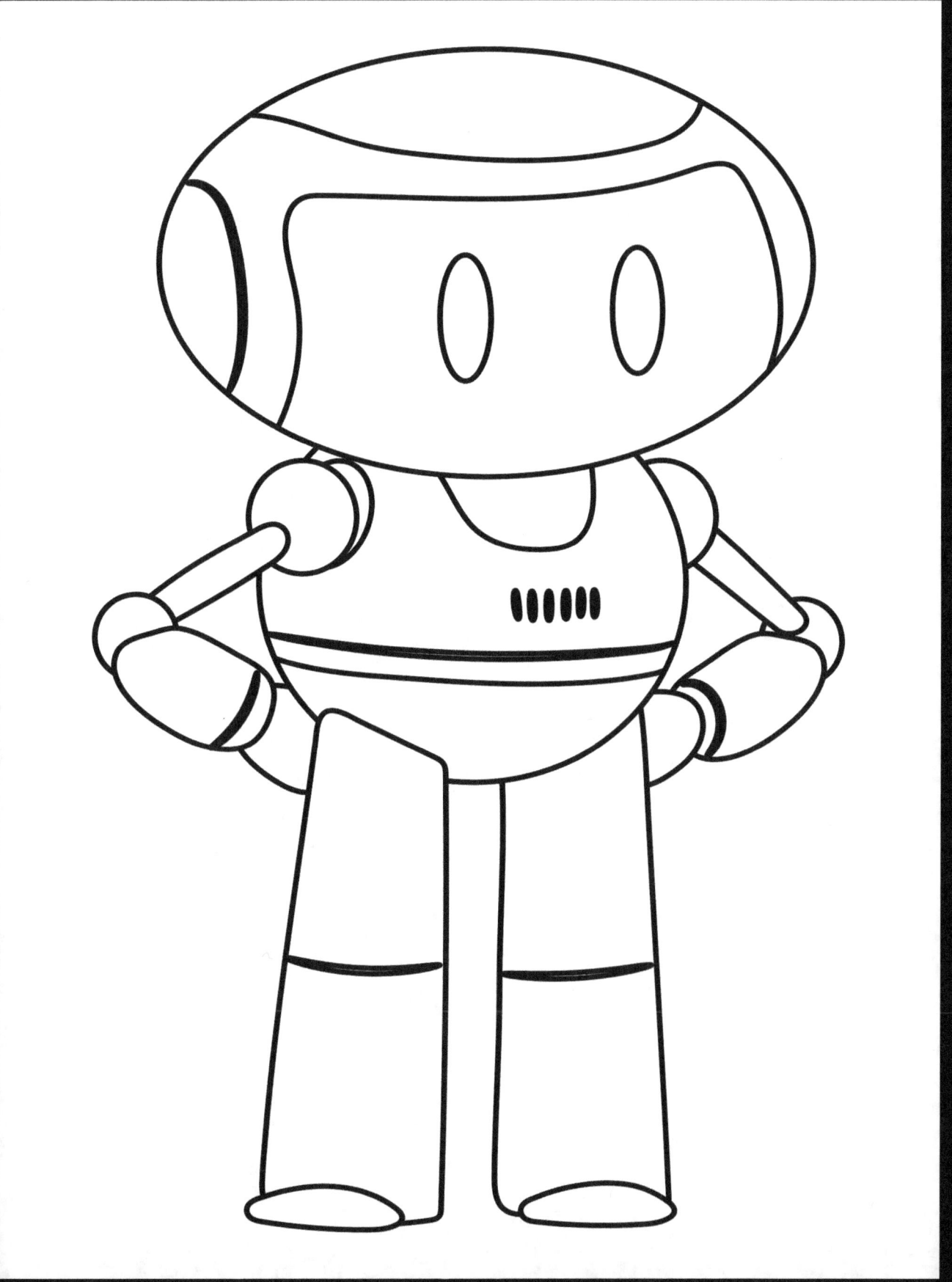

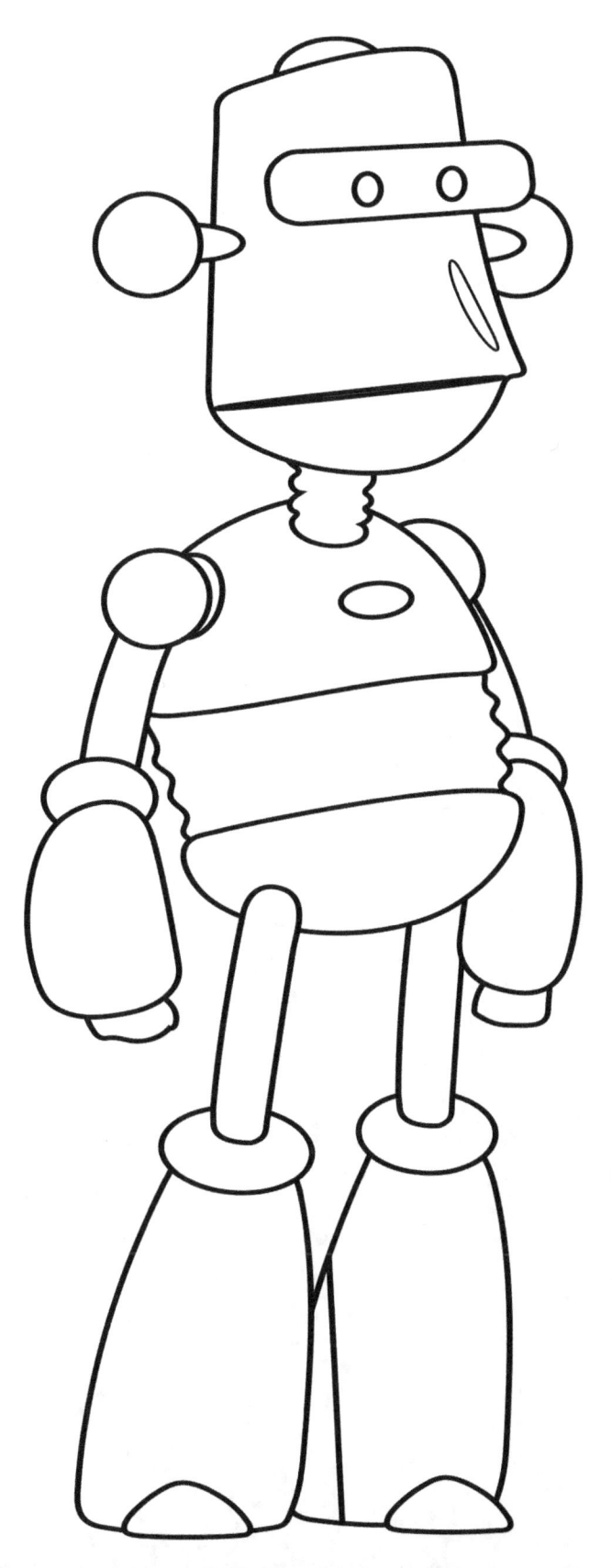

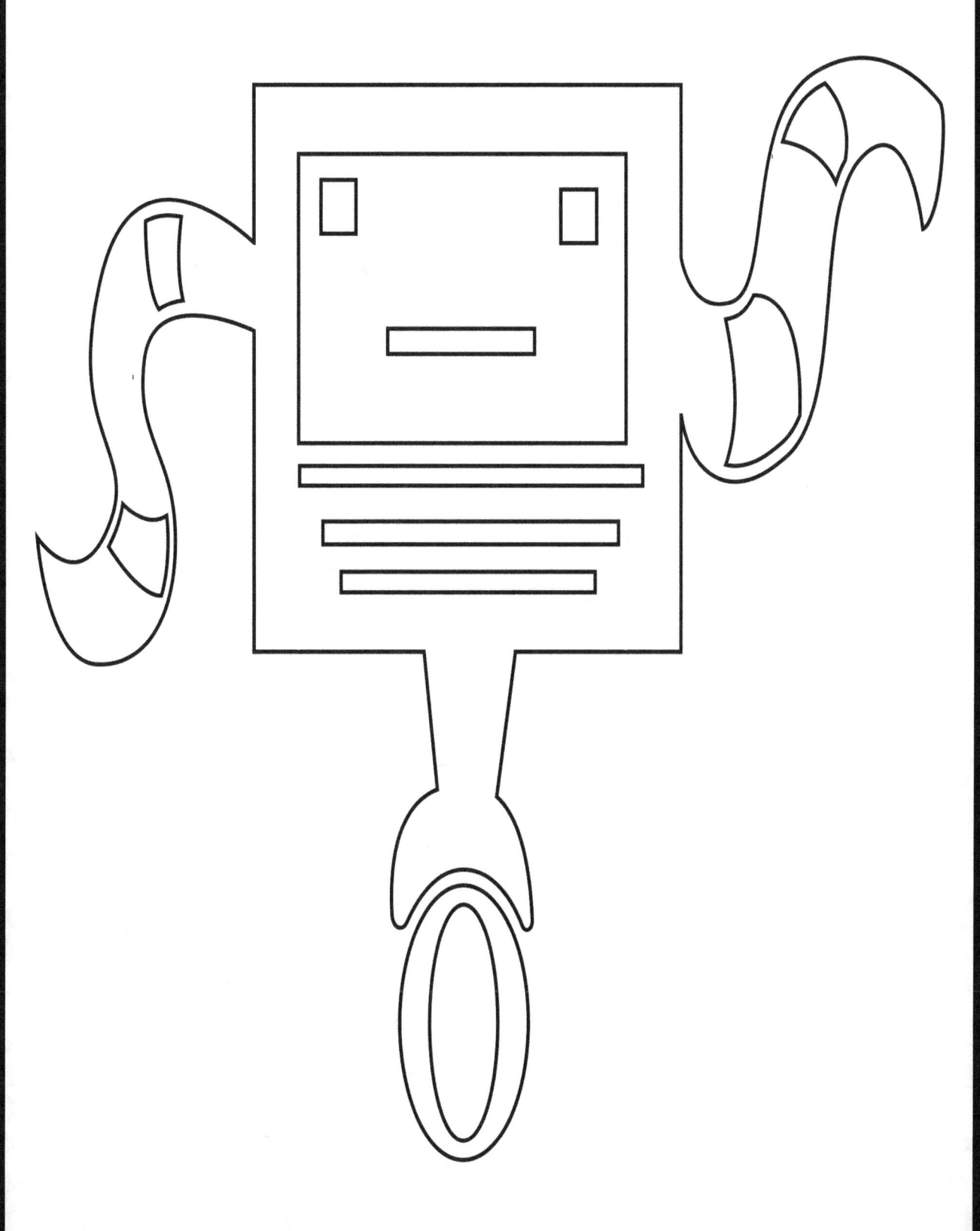

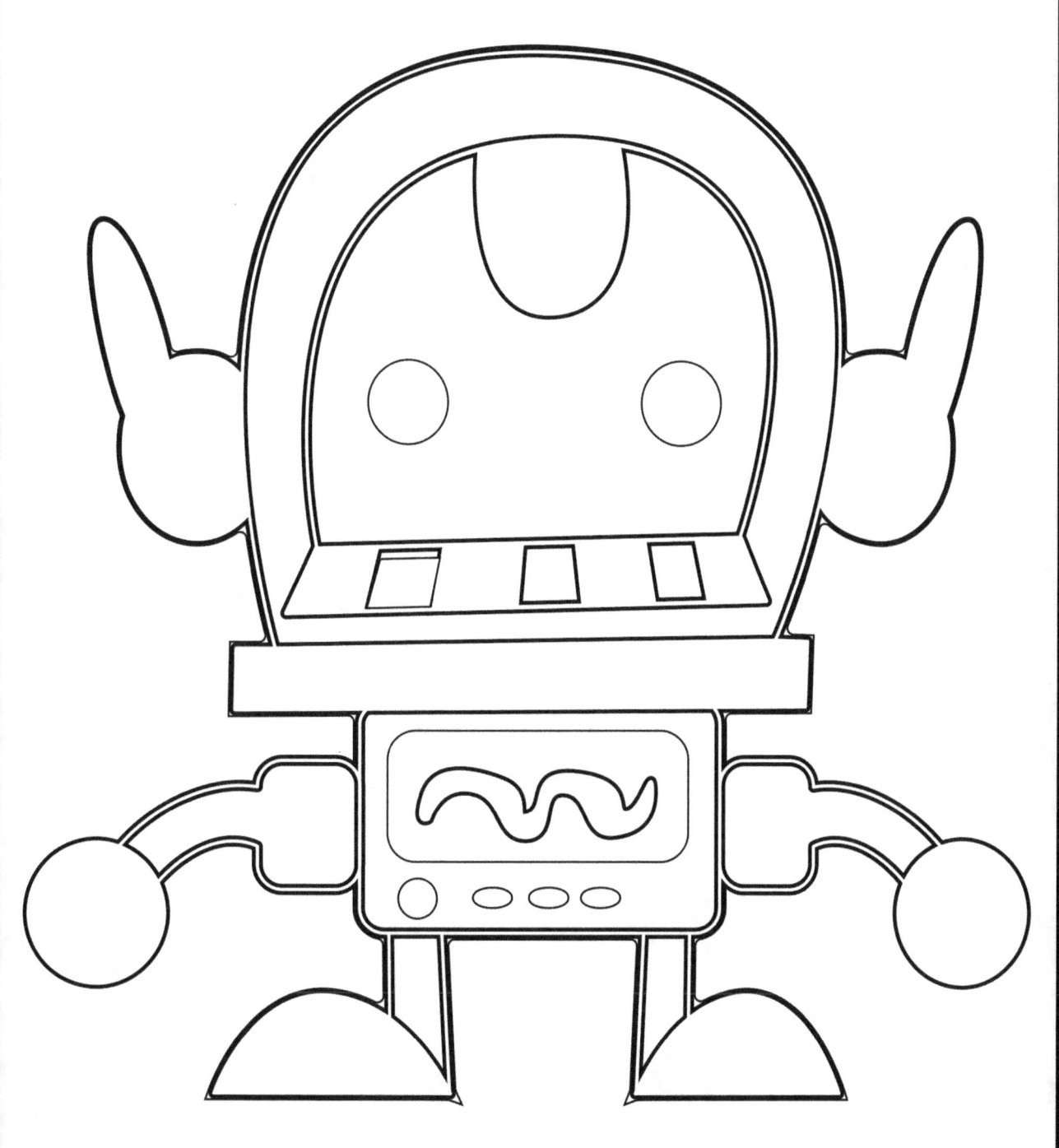

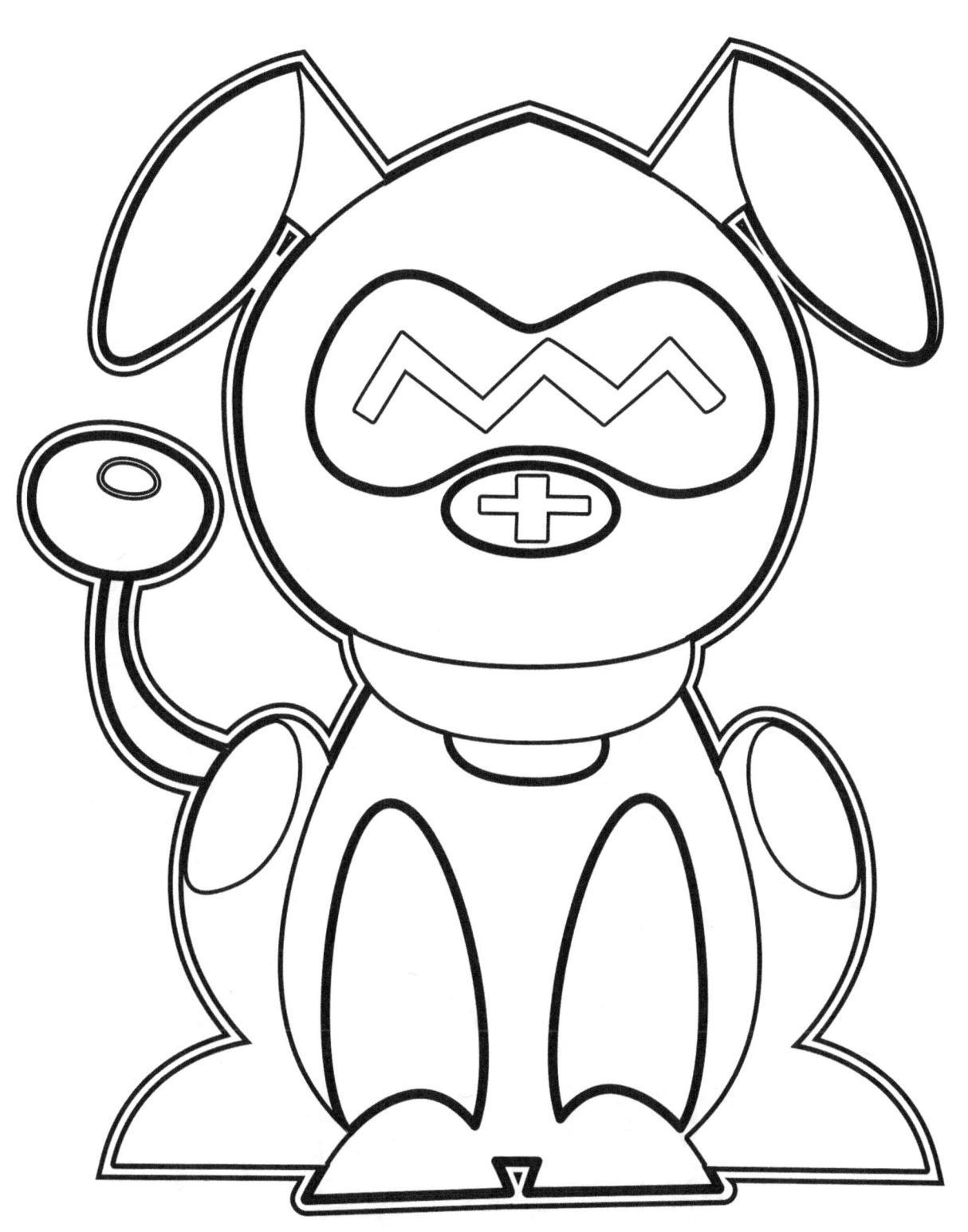

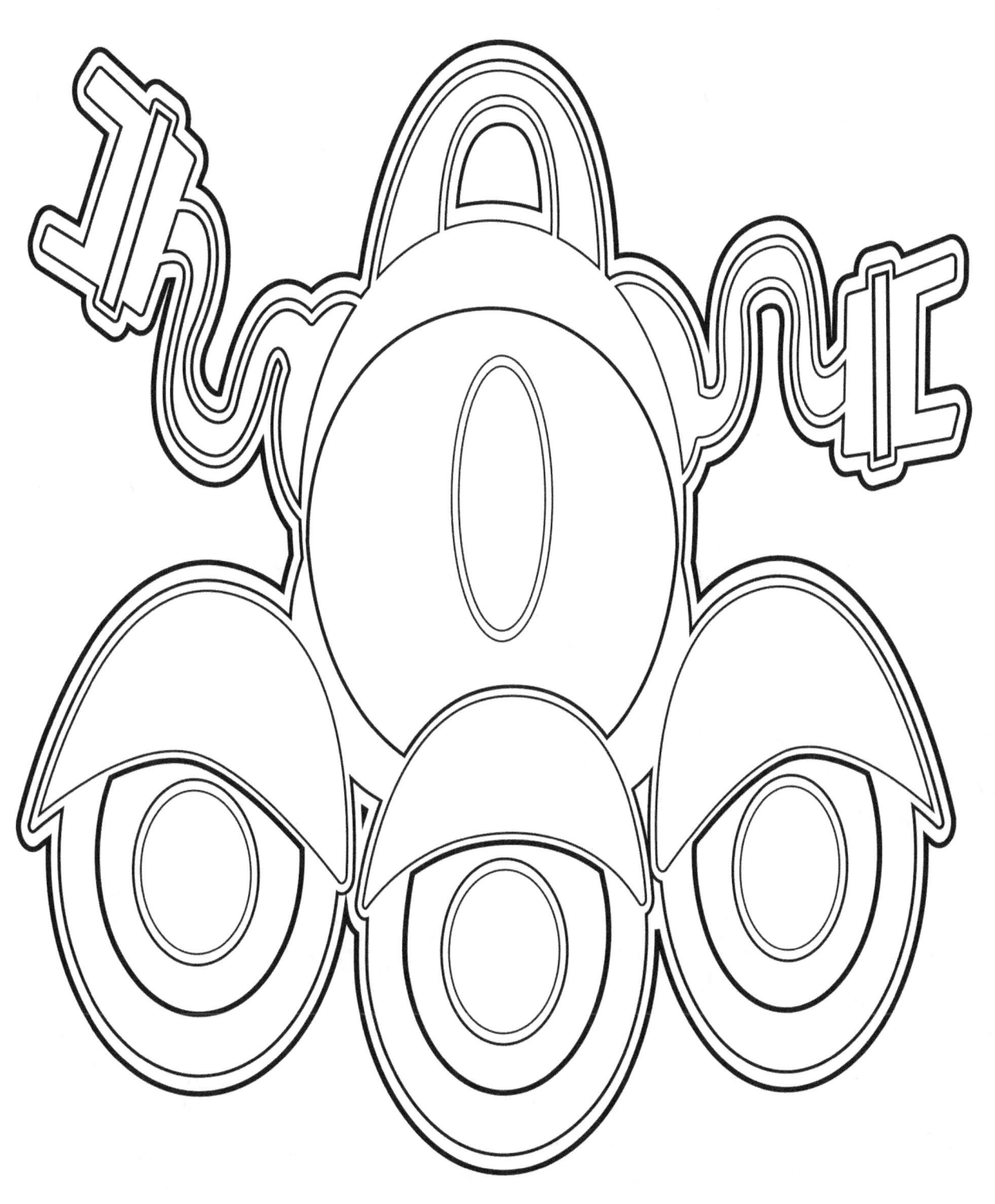

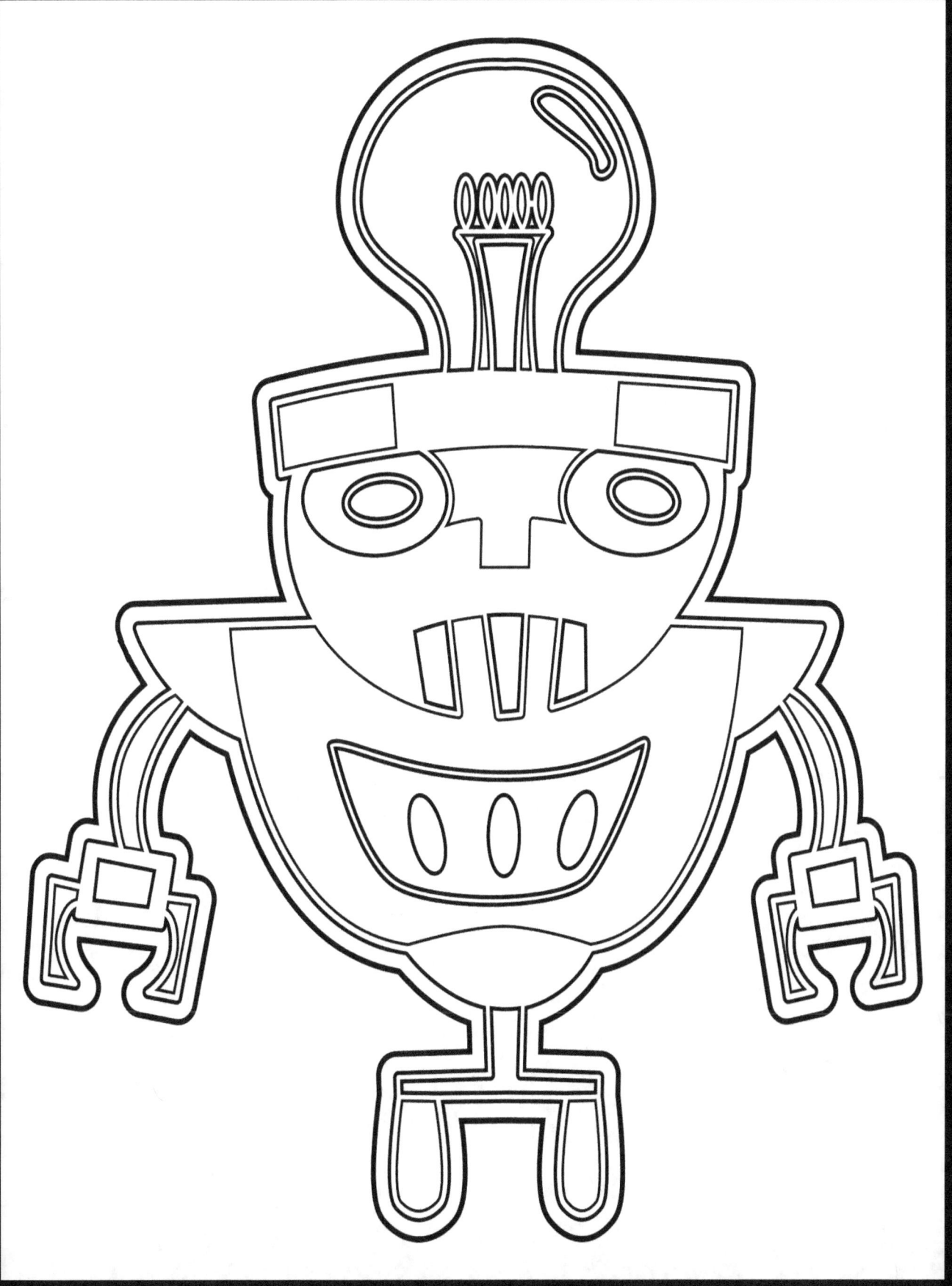

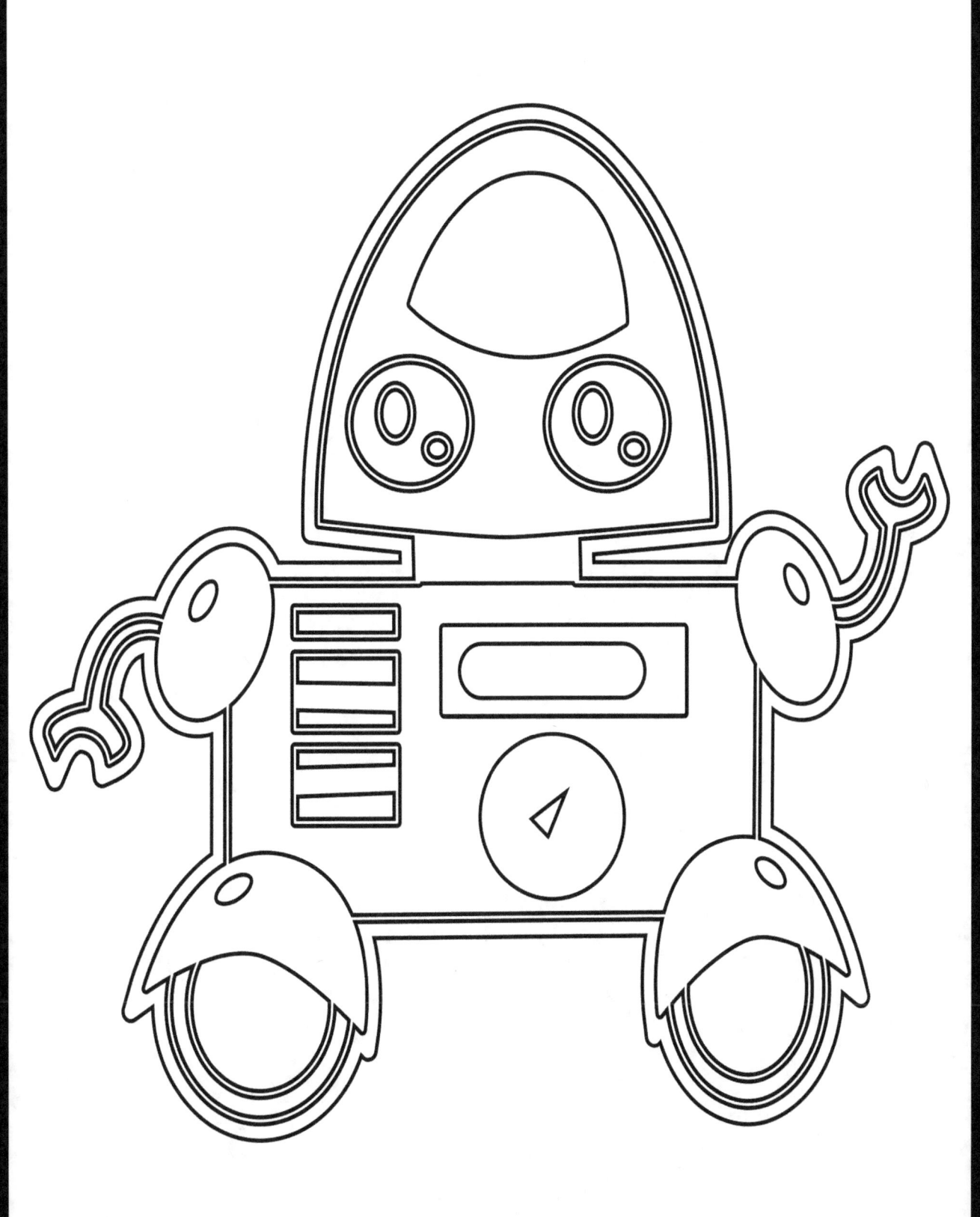

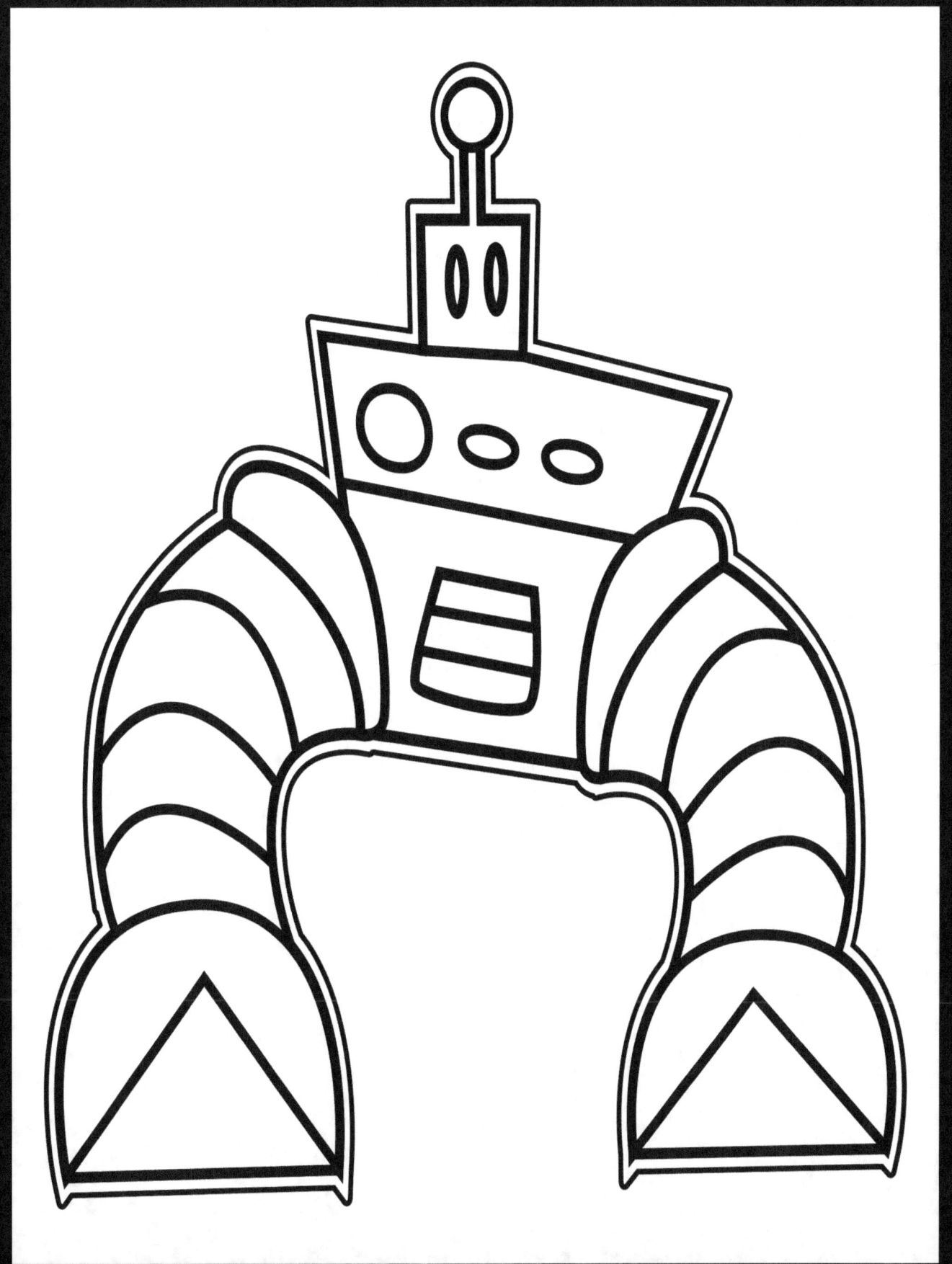

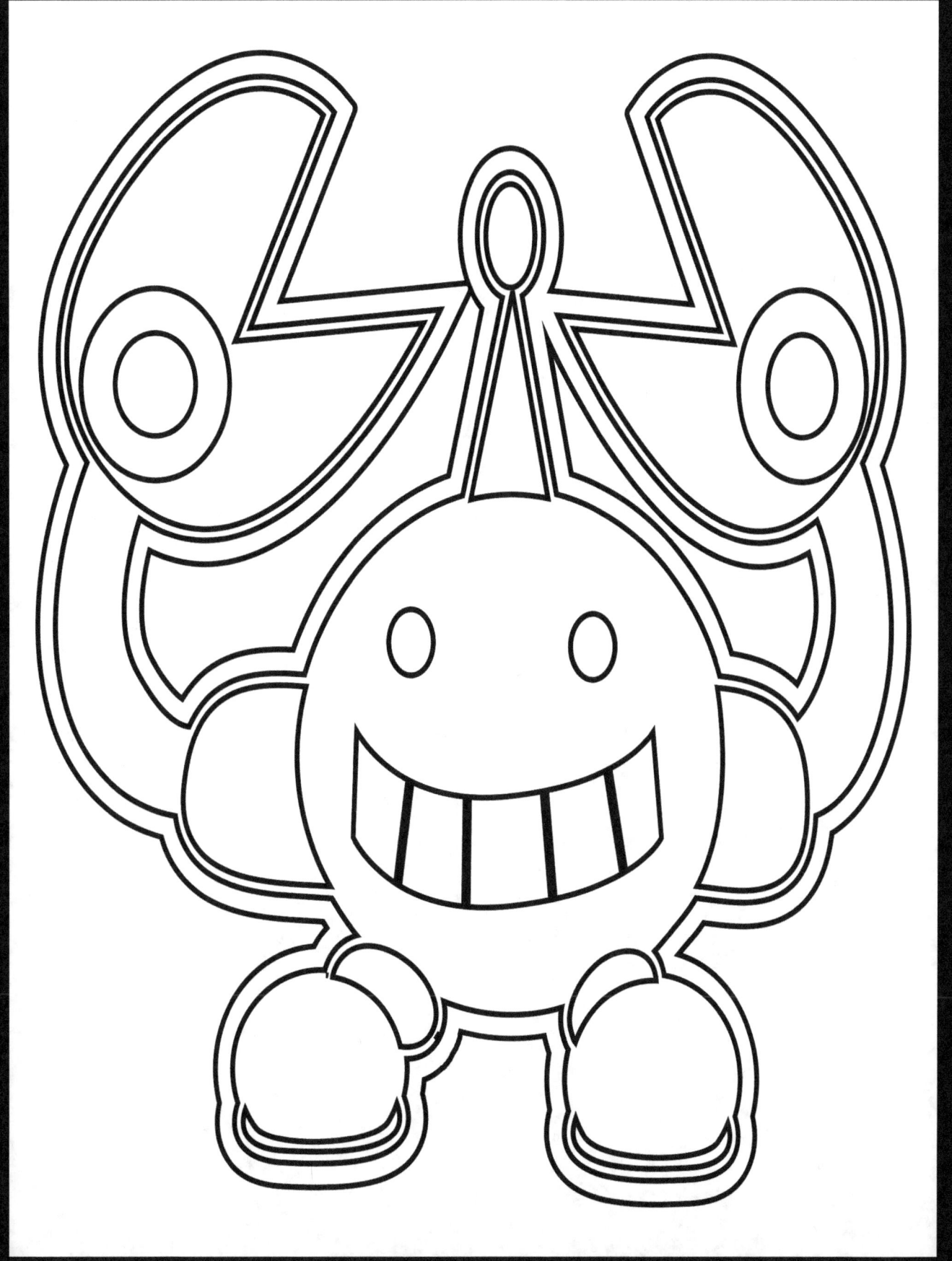

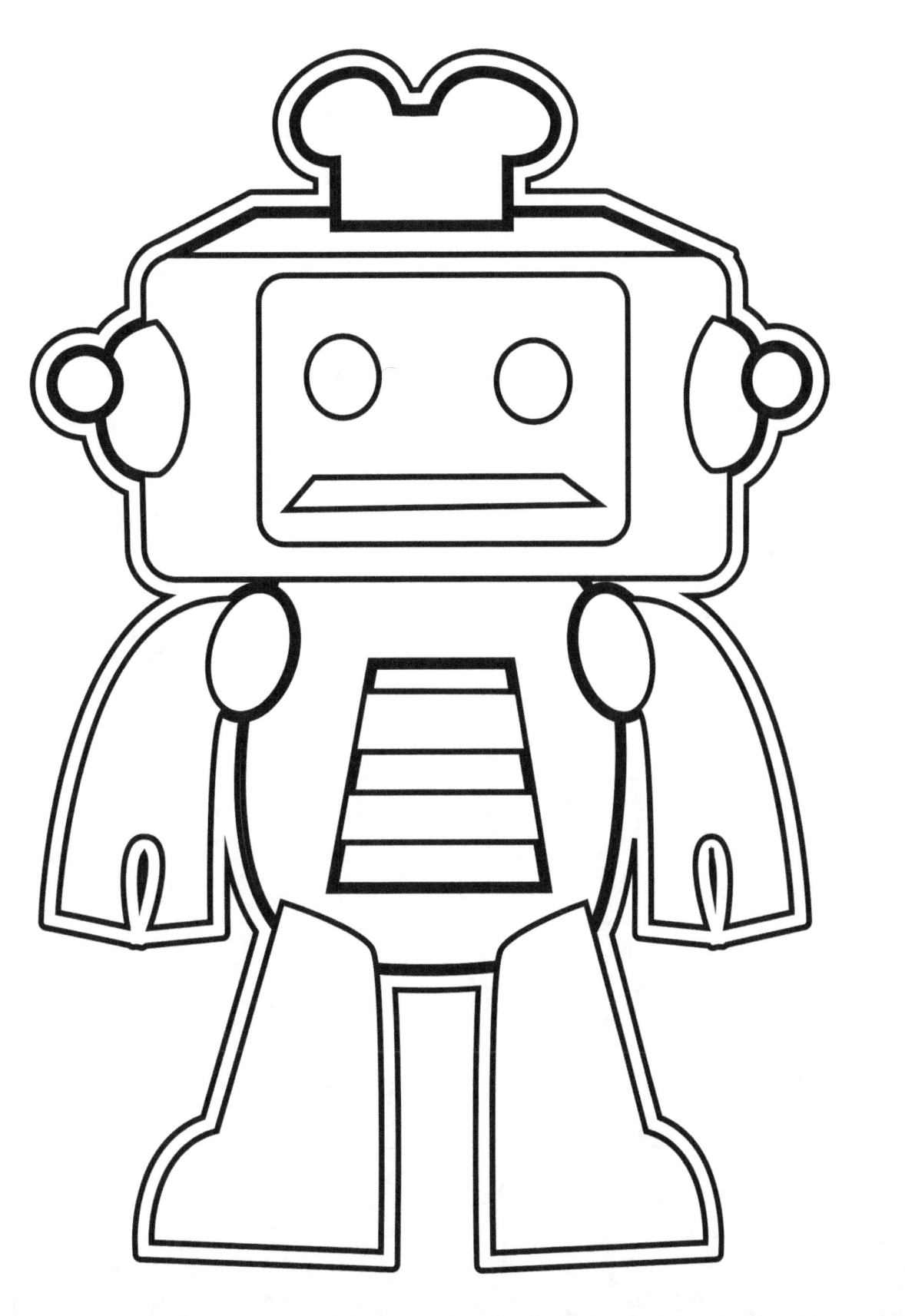

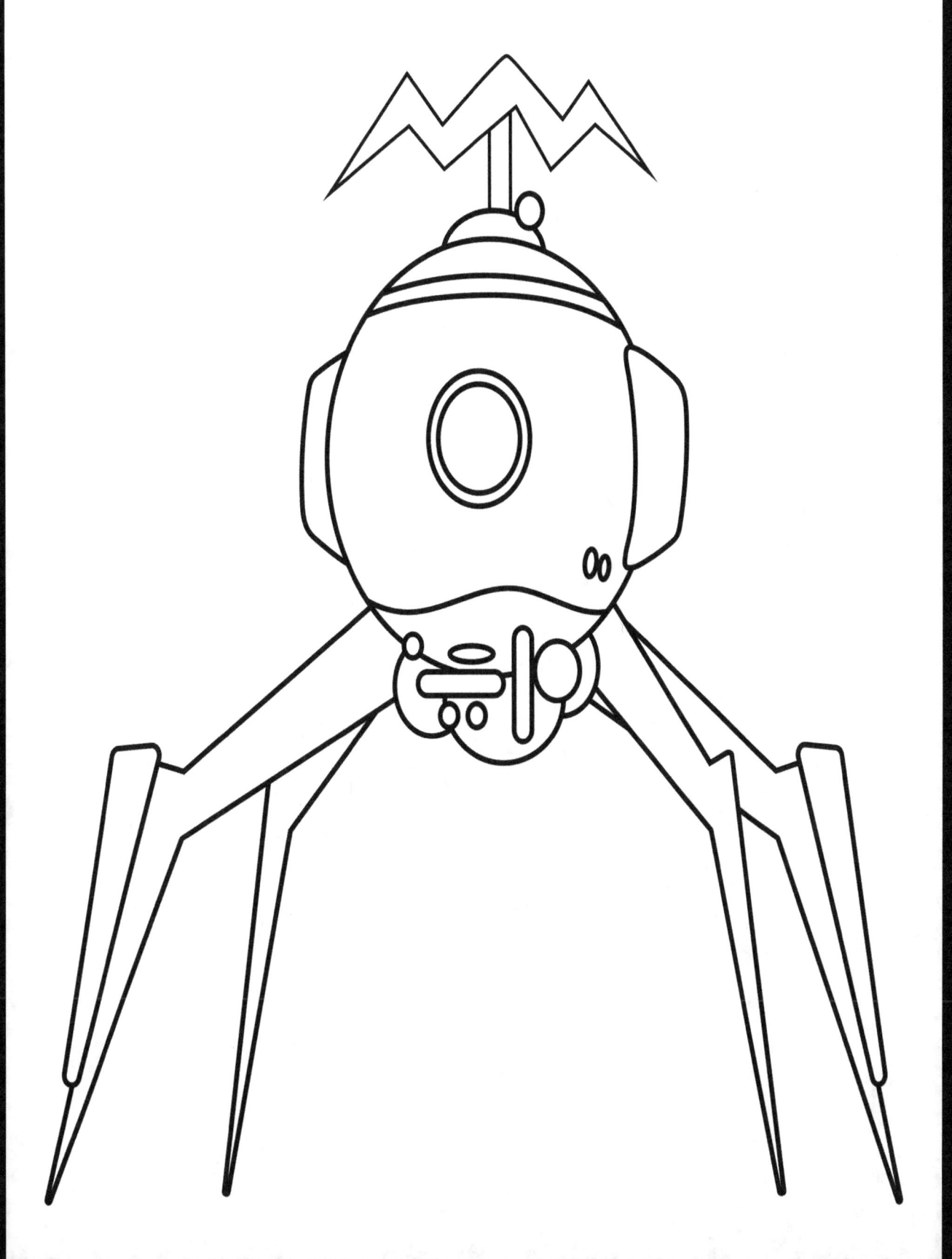

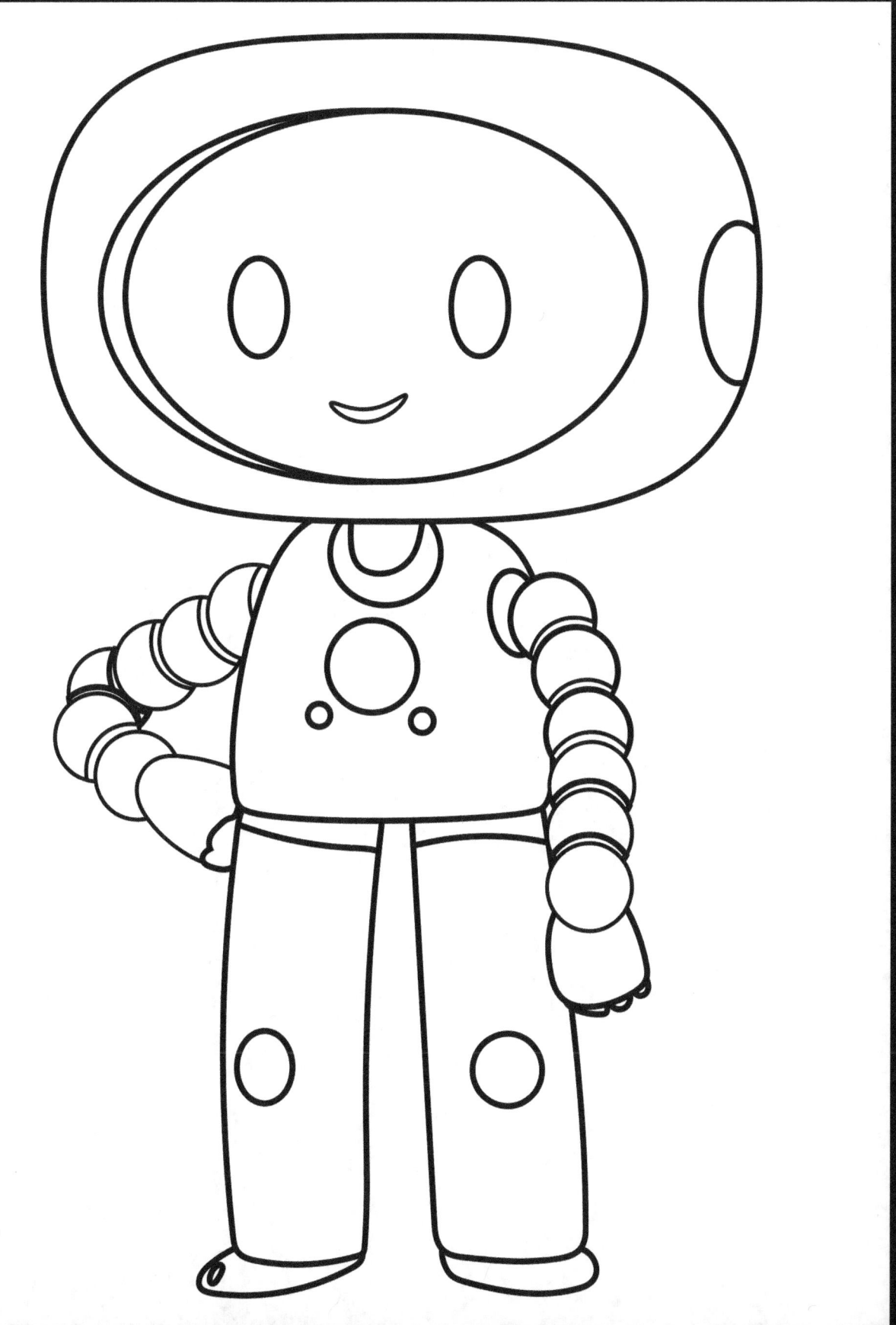

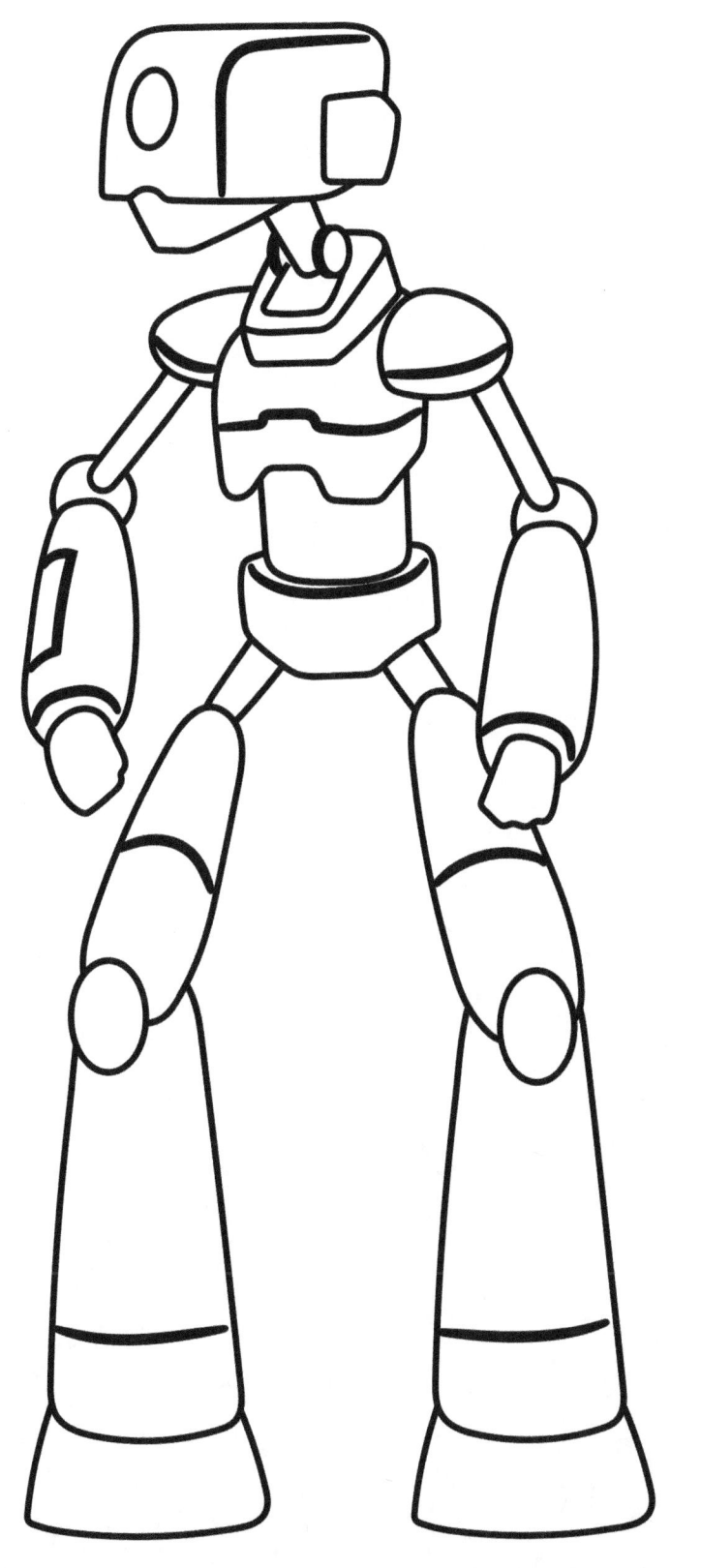

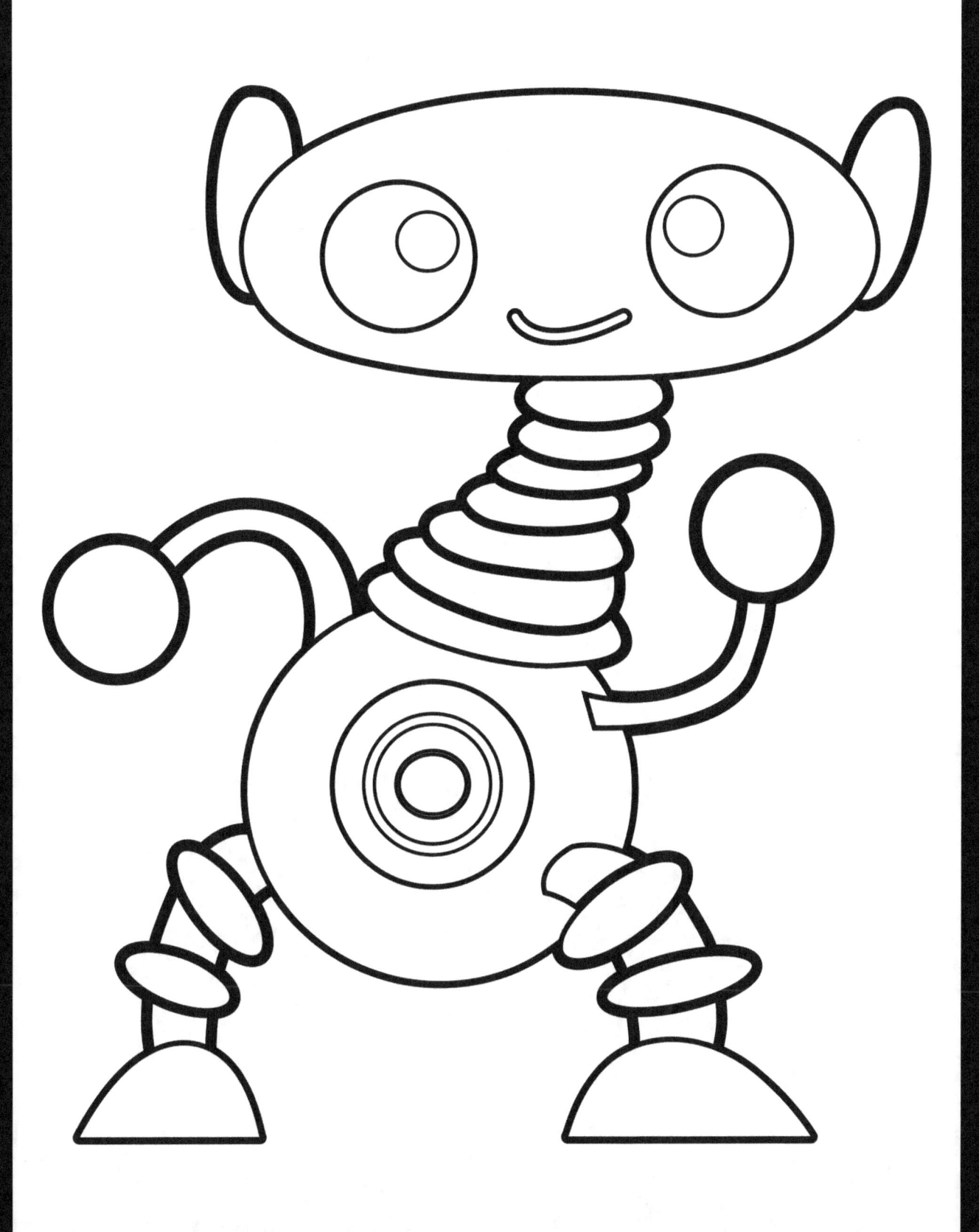

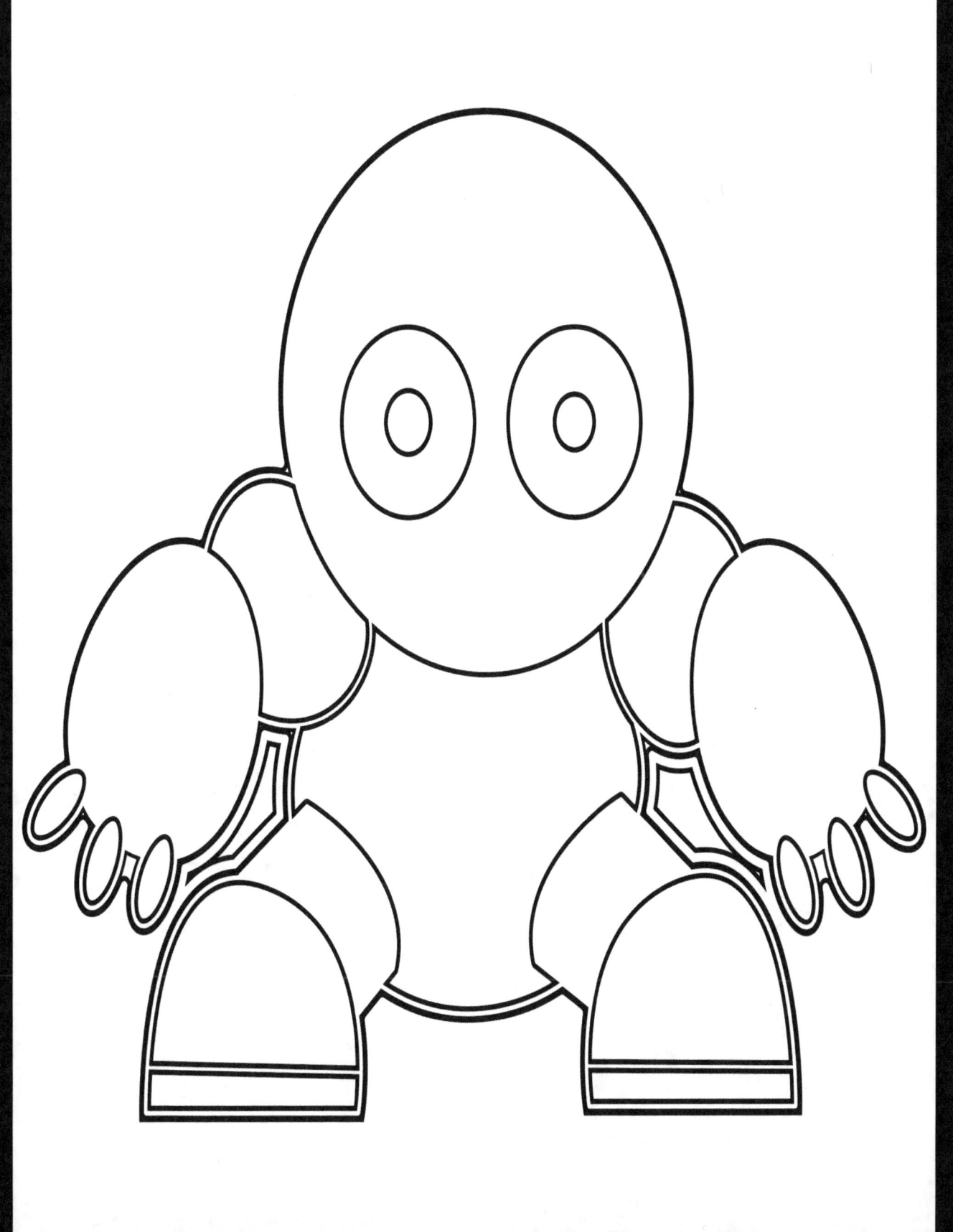

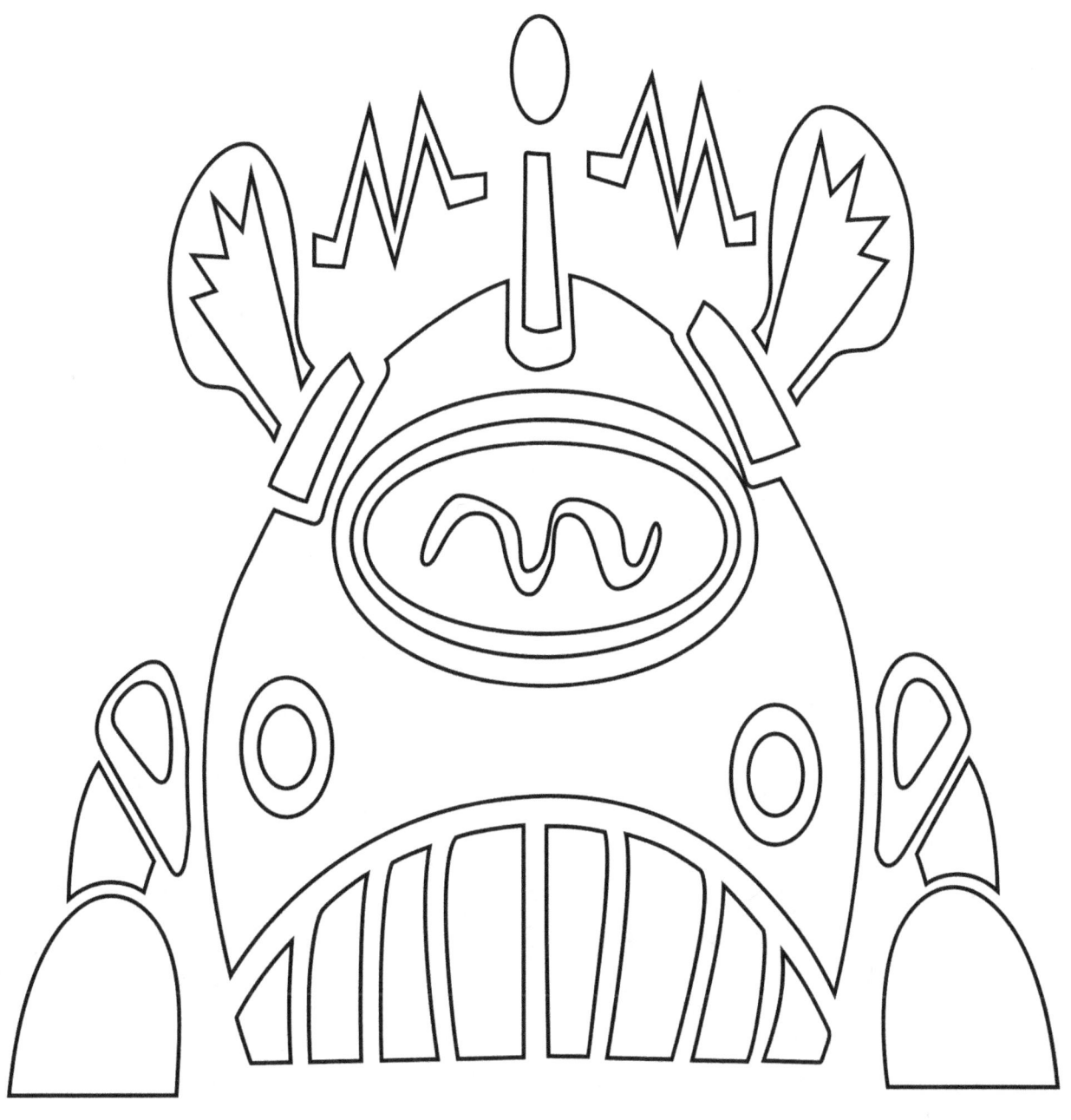

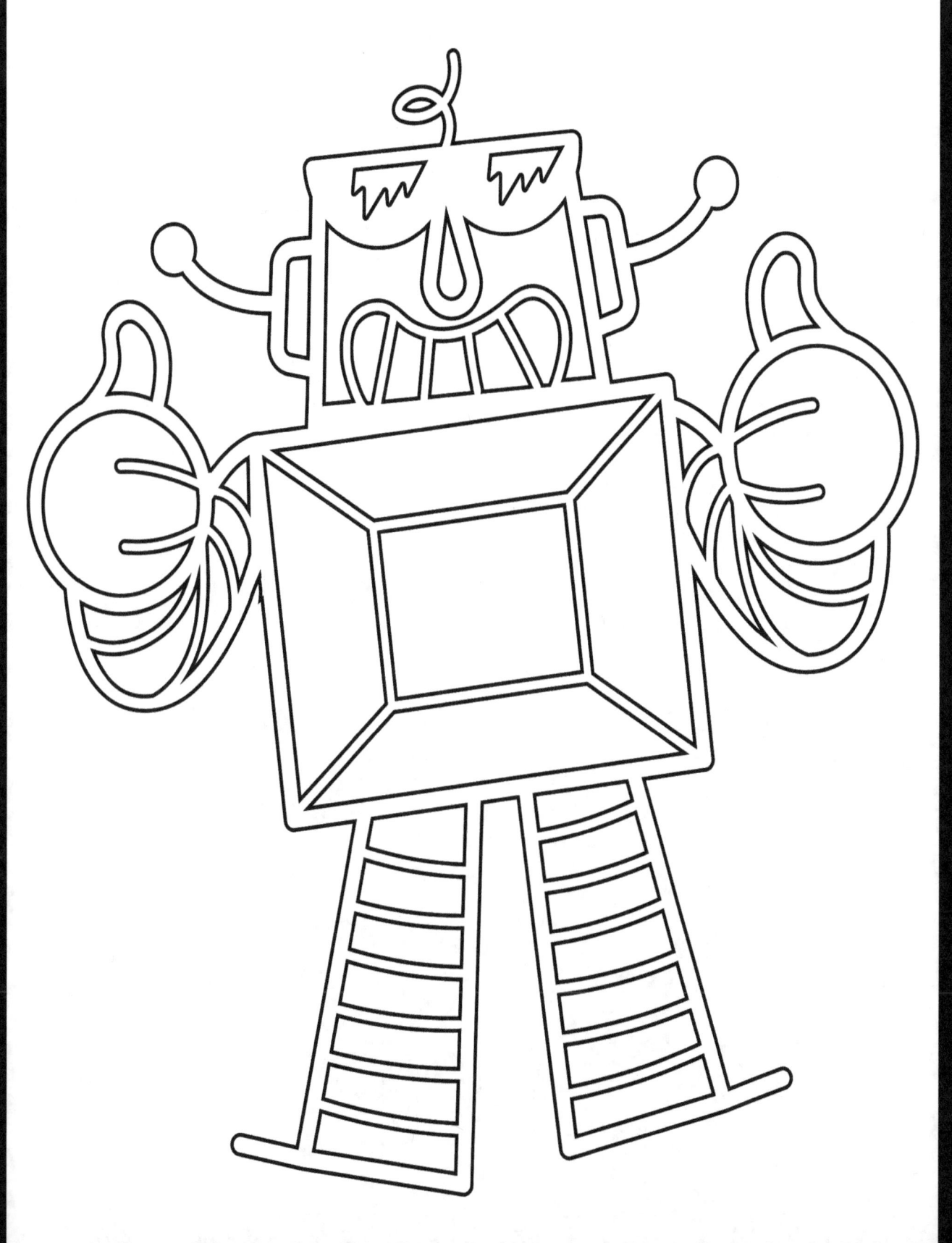

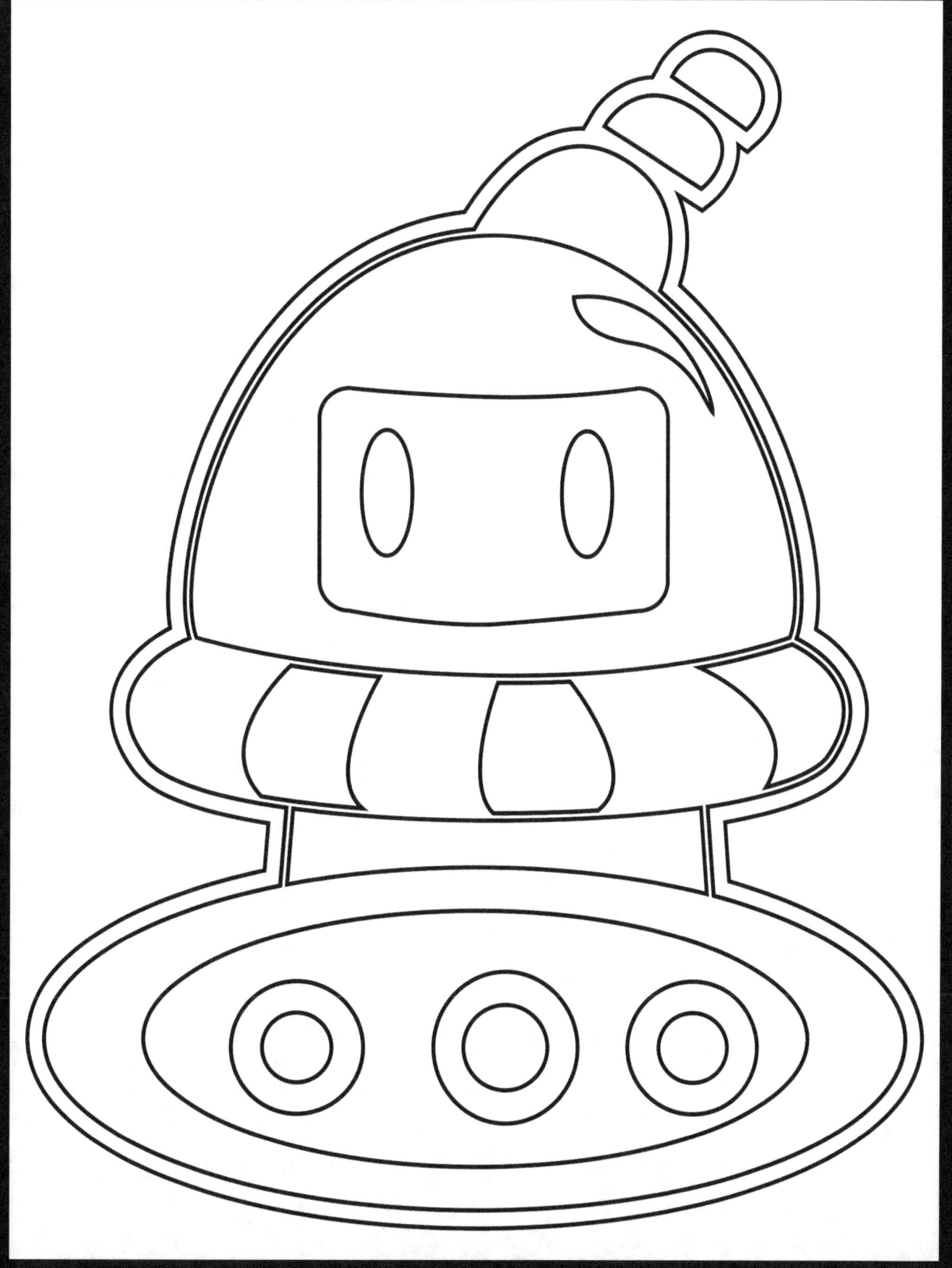

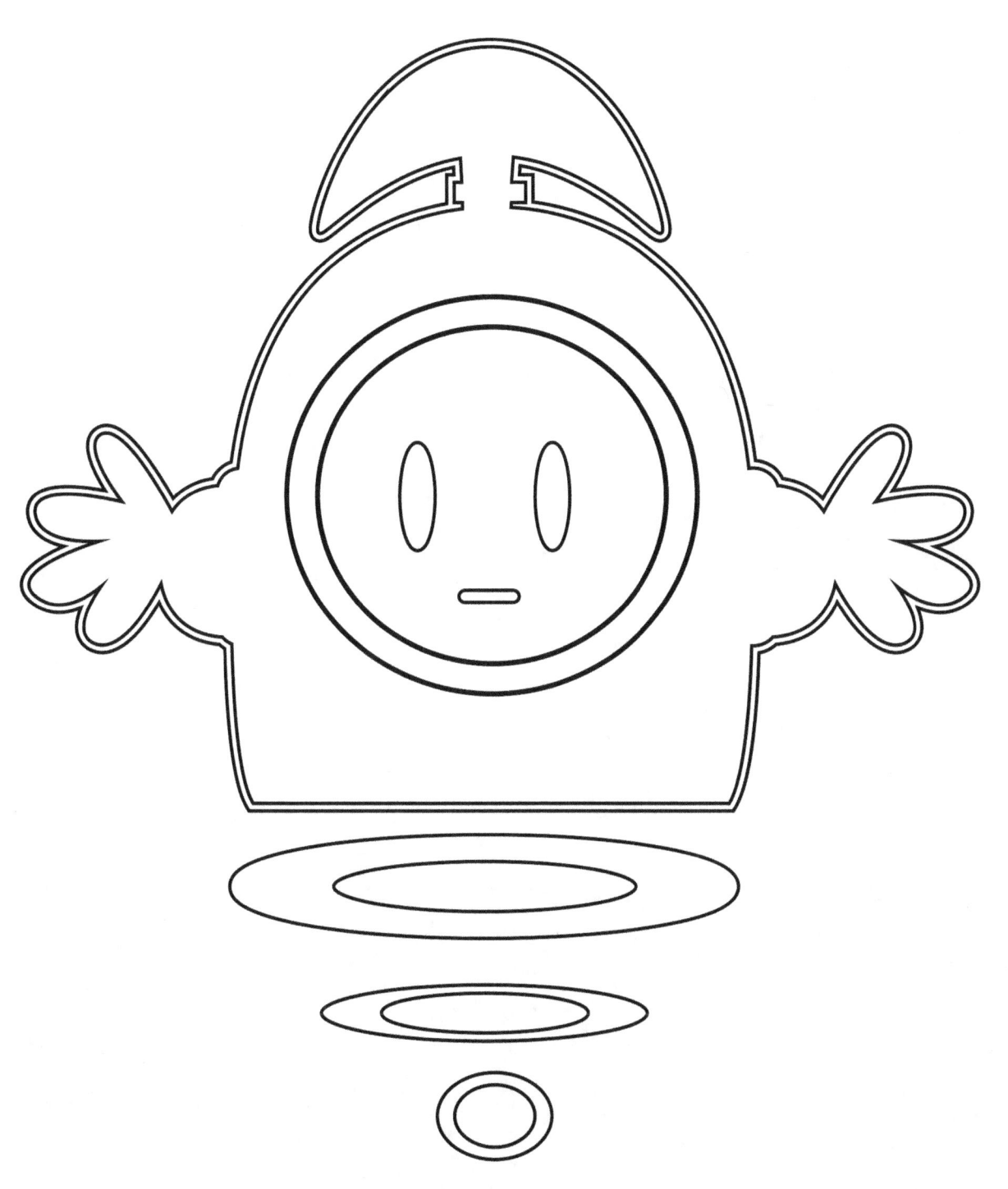

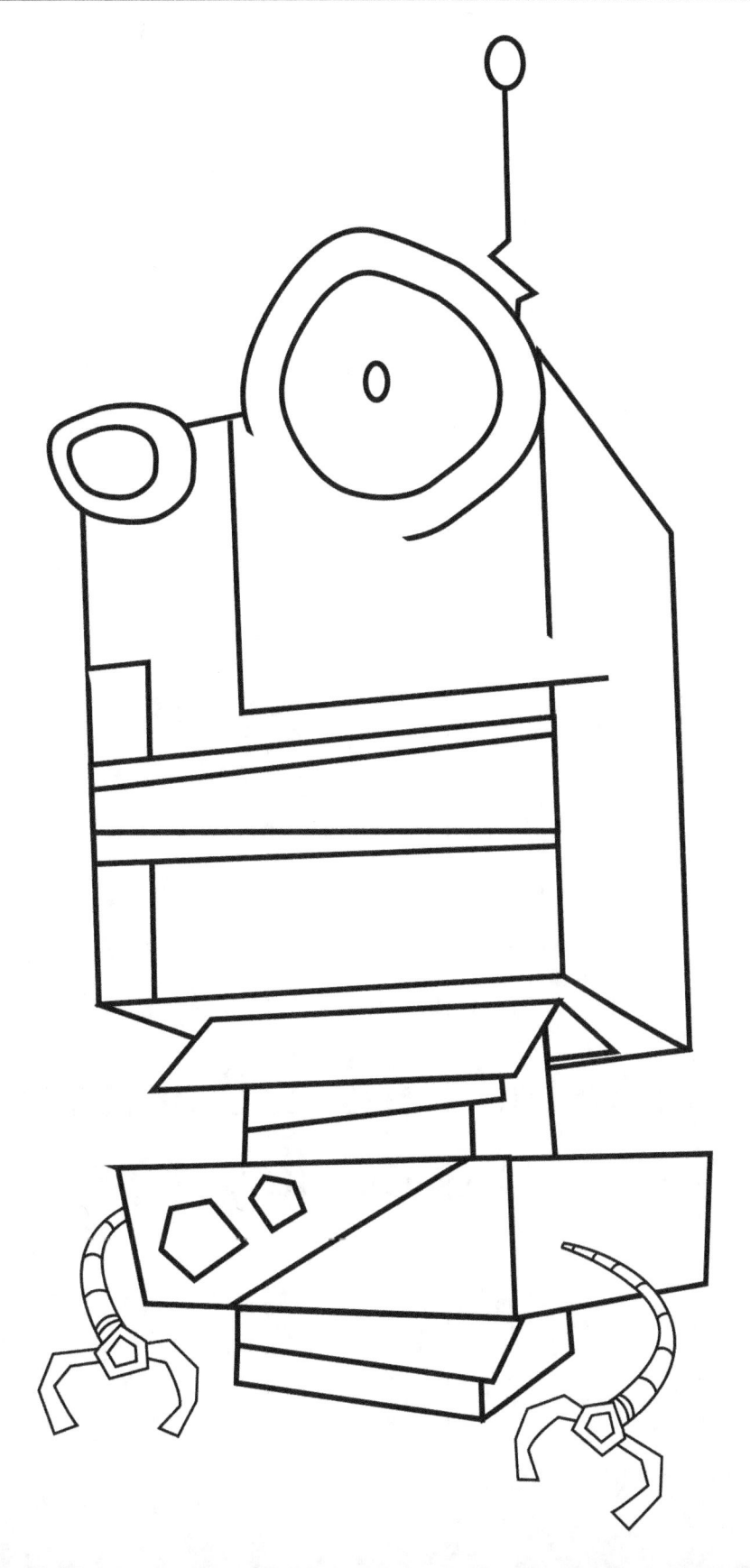

I hope you like the book and enjoyed it, Have a good day.